THE BAPTISM
&
THE TOILET

BY LEROI JONES

GW00645505

GROVE PRESS, INC.
New York

THE BAPTISM

The Baptism was first presented by Present Stages at the Writers' Stage Theatre, New York, on March 23, 1964. It was directed by Jerry Benjamin, designed by Joe Brainard, with lights by Nicola Cernovich and Janet Castle, and costumes by Gertha. The cast was as follows:

BOY .... Russell Turman

MINISTER .... Jarrett Spruill

HOMOSEXUAL .... Taylor Mead

OLD WOMAN .... Beverly Grant

MESSENGER .... Mark Duffy

WOMEN .... Jacquelyn Colton, Colette
Hawks, Marilyn Lee, Marie
Clair Charba, Joanne
Hargarther, Susan Shawn

ABOUT THE AUTHOR

LEROI JONES was born in Newark, New Jersey, in 1934. He attended Rutgers University, Howard University, Columbia University, and The New School. A poet, novelist, and essayist, as well as a playwright, he has published, among other works, *The Dead Lecturer* (poems), *The System of Dante's Hell* (novel), and *Home: Social Essays*. His play, *Dutchman,* won the Obie Award for the Best American Play of the 1963–1964 season. He was the founder and director of the Black Arts Repertory Theatre/School in Harlem.

EVERGREEN PLAYSCRIPT No. 10

THE BAPTISM
&
THE TOILET

CHARACTERS

BOY: *15 or so. Handsome, almost to girlishness. Martyr-like shyness, sometimes feigned.*

MINISTER: *Black robe, white-haired, pompous, appears well meaning, generally ridiculous.*

WOMEN: *Young sleek "Village!" types.*

OLD WOMAN: *Strong from years of the American Matriarchy. Loud.*

HOMOSEXUAL: *Elegant, 40-ish, priggish,* soi-disant *intellectual. Growing fat around the middle and extremely conscious of it. Very queenly.*

MESSENGER: *Motorcycle stereotype. Can be Spanish or resemble Lee Marvin.*

*An almost well-to-do arrogant Protestant church, obviously
Baptist. Most of the action takes place on the altar. A huge
white cross of glass is dangled from the ceiling at the rear of
the altar with the inscription "IHS" written on the crossbar.
The decor is mostly red velvet and gold. A speaker's stand is
at the front of the dais, and 2 microphones stand in front of it.
The inscription "IHS" is written on the speaker stand as well.
Under this inscription a plaque that says "WHBI RADIO."*

MINISTER: Break the chain of ignorance. Lord, in his high
place. What returns to us, images, the tone of death. Our
cloak of color, our love for ourselves and our hymns. *(Moves
to center of the stage bowing, with folded hands at his chin.)*
Not love. *(Moans.)* Not love. The betrayed music. Stealth.
We rise to the tops of our buildings and they name them after
us. We take off our hoods *(removes red hood)* and show our
eyes. I am holy father of silence. *(Kneels.)*

HOMOSEXUAL: Not love. *(Moans.)* Not love. The man kneeling is only suppliant. Tarzan of the apes of religion. Lothar
in the world. Weakling and non-swimmer. Manager of the
Philadelphia Phillies. Not a good person to sleep with.
Gags on all flesh. The flesh hung in our soft sleep. That
thin Jewish cowboy.

MINISTER *(rising, doing slow dance step with leg raised)*:
Precious. Precious. This is a deception. A laggardly
music, again, that image. *(Leaps.)* The place of the soul,
my kindly queen, is wherever it rests. I fuck no one who
does not claim to love me. You are less selective.

HOMOSEXUAL: *(starting to run in place)*: Action. Camera.
(Stops.) Stop! Stop! Where are my critics? Where are my
father's friends with their bowling bags? I refuse to make a
spectacle of religion without my most perceptive allies

present. *(Raises arm.)* We will speak of politics or be forever silent.

MINISTER *(running in place)*: The place of the soul is its virtue. It is man's music. His move from flesh. When you are strapped in sin, I pray for you, dear queen. I stare with X-ray eyes into your dark room and suffer with you. I smell your lovers, and pray that you be redeemed. I bathe them in my holy water, and they are as baptized children.

HOMOSEXUAL: You are filthy with success, you religious motherfucker. Who, may I ask, is your tailor?

The BOY *enters, in a black robe, with a bag on his back.*

MINISTER *(pointing)*: Here comes the boy. The gentle soul who comes to be baptized.

HOMOSEXUAL: Looks like rough trade to me.

BOY *(looking up with feigned humility)*: Father, pray for me. *(Kneels quickly, sobbing.)* Father, pray for me. I've sinned. *(Weeps and sprawls on floor.)*

MINISTER: Love?

HOMOSEXUAL *(in stage whisper)*: You, sir, are an opportunist.

BOY: Father, help me, I've sinned.

MINISTER *(kneels to comfort* BOY*)*: Raise your head, my son. Nothing puts you outside of God's wisdom and mercy. Ours is a God of charity.

HOMOSEXUAL *starts running in place, stops, drops trousers to reveal red leotards.*

12

BOY (*looking over Minister's shoulder at* HOMOSEXUAL):
Father, you must help me. I've sinned. And I was to be
baptized today. (*His attention begins to wander.*) Father. . .

MINISTER (*looking around to see what the disturbance is.
Rushes at* HOMOSEXUAL *and they scuffle*): You've cheated
in the collections. Withheld the beautiful money of the poor.
Shouted the chorales out of key, and groped the organist in
the trustees' room.

HOMOSEXUAL (*with dignity*): I am the Son of Man. (*Wrests
himself away from* MINISTER *and does ballet step.*) I've done
nothing not accounted for in the book of days. Come judg-
ment, Dick, let's see how easy you get off.

BOY: Father, will you bless me? Will you wipe my sin away?

HOMOSEXUAL *assumes exaggerated position and watches
the* BOY *haughtily.*

MINISTER: My son, if the Lord is with you, you need not fear.

HOMOSEXUAL: No one but you, my sutler. My vision of bleak-
ness. My interminable liar, executioner of the ignorant.

MINISTER (*turning to* HOMOSEXUAL): You are becoming un-
pleasant Miss Cocksucker and I don't like it.

OLD WOMAN (*rushing into church and toward dais*): That boy!
That boy! He sinned! I watched him. He committed a vile
crime against the laws of our Saviour. The Lord, who was
resurrected. Who, himself, died for us. Was butchered and
lived low with thieves and Jews and had little or no money
and walked everywhere He had to go. Saviour! (*Kneels, praying, then rises screaming.*) That boy! That lad, there.
Agent of the devil.

13

HOMOSEXUAL: Noisy old Christian ain't you?

OLD WOMAN *(startled)*: God is noisier. And none of us can be too noisy in his behalf. It was the silence of ignorance and the silence of greed that had us expelled from the Lord's house. Sin is a stealthy beast.

HOMOSEXUAL: No style to you sister.

MINISTER: Bless you all, my children. Be quiet that you may experience the Lord's word. *(Turns to* BOY.*)* My son, what have you to say in answer to this devout woman's accusations?

BOY *(casually, like confident criminal)*: I never saw her before in my life.

OLD WOMAN: You lie. I saw you with the Lord's own eyes. I watched your depravity. I sat in my kitchen and watched you in your bedroom kneeling, pretending to pray. I saw.

BOY: You watched me kneeling?

OLD WOMAN: Yes. Yes. For the Lord had bade me to do so.

BOY: I was praying.

OLD WOMAN: You are from hell. You are of the evil place. I watched you kneel as if to pray. . .and then you blasphemed the Lord. *(She begins to run in place, bowing to the empty pews. Then she begins to take off her diverse aprons and skirts, all the time trying to continue running.)* Saints! Saints! The naked virtue of Your creation. The virgin of truth. I cast the stone, because of Your son's virtue. To root the sinners out. Make a list, Lord, make a list of them. And I'll root them out, and cast them in the pit.

14

BOY *(screams)*: I was praying.

MINISTER: Not love. *(Moans.)* Not love. Prayer. You were praying and the Lord will respond. You are not lost my son. If you are true and clean and ambitious, the Lord will not pass you by.

HOMOSEXUAL: He needs a job, holy father. And I need a secretary.

MINISTER: Son, there are no temptations for the wise man. The sins of the flesh, are not the sins of the leopard. Cast down your lies and fall on me praying.

HOMOSEXUAL *(ballet steps. Takes colored confetti from his pocket and tosses it over the assembly. Sings)*: The pride of life is life. And flesh must make its move. I am the sinister lover of love. The mysterious villain of thought. I love my mind, my asshole too. I love all things. As they are issued from you know who. God. God. God. God. Go-od. The great insouciant dilettante. My lovers, priests, immolated queers, how many other worlds are there, less happy, less sorrowful than ours? God. God. God. God. Go-od. The thug of creation. Our holy dilettante.

MINISTER: Cast down your sins *(embraces the* BOY*)* and fall on me praying. We will enter the streets of the city blessing the wretched and preaching the word of the Lord. Fall on me, oh my son. Fall on me praying.

OLD WOMAN: He sinned. He sinned. He sinned. *(Screams, jumping and pointing like a witch.)* I saw him. I watched him kneel and blaspheme our God. Sin. Sin. A demon of hot flesh. *(Settling, but still screaming, growing more intent and moved by what she is recounting.)* Sin. He closed his eyes. The lashes fluttered. And I saw how strong he thought to be.

Sin. He took that member in his hand. With the other hand under his chin as if in profile to pray. And I watched the eyelids flutter. As a soft bird will. His black hair sparkling on his ears. And his lips moving slowly with that flutter of eyelids for our Lord. BLASPHEMER. *(She runs to strike the* **BOY***, and the* **MINISTER** *protects him, brushing his hair softly and tenderly.)* BLASPHEMER. You spilled your seed while pretending to talk to God. I saw you. That quick short stroke. And it was so soft before, and you made it grow in your hand. I watched it stiffen, and your lips move and those short hard moves with it straining in your fingers for flesh. Not God. You spilled the seed in God's name? And then that fluid, what all life needs, spilled there in your fingers, and your lips still moving begging God to forgive you. *(She falls on her knees before the* **BOY***.)* You blaspheme. *(She is running down, growing softer. She holds the Minister's robe, running her hand around it to get to the* **BOY***.)* Your wet sticky hand. I watched you smell it, with your eyes closed and mouth still moving for the Lord. That hand, where so much life was stilled. And you held it to your nose, and put the fingers in your mouth. You blaspheme. The flesh. My God. Those lovely eyelids moving. That hand placed so. Just so, and there was light coming over your shoulder all through your long hair. My lovely, lovely youth. *(She collapses trying to grasp the Boy's legs.)*

MINISTER *(still stroking the Boy's head)*: She has swooned in the service of the Lord. A holy ecstasy has entered her soul.

HOMOSEXUAL *(turns her over with his toe)*: Hmm, I think maybe she's had a bit too much to drink.

MINISTER: The Lord is with you also my son. Is what the woman said true?

BOY: Yes, father. I could not help it. Thinking of God always gives me a hard-on.

HOMOSEXUAL *(the ballet step. Humming his song. Stops)*: Do you dance, lad?

BOY: Yes sir. I know the popular steps of the day.

HOMOSEXUAL: Will you dance with me?

BOY: In church?

MINISTER *(to* HOMOSEXUAL*)*: Do you have no respect for this place of holy works.

HOMOSEXUAL: Yes. I envy you your brilliant cover story. Dance with me, lad. *(Extends both hands.)*

BOY: I cannot. It is a holy place. I cannot blaspheme twice in the same afternoon.

MINISTER: This is a gifted lad. You cannot sway him with your cant about religion or the evil pleasures of the flesh. He has seen what evil the body is. You cannot move him.

OLD WOMAN *(starts to stir. Begins humming, then singing quietly)*: Leaning. Leaning. Leaning on the everlasting light.

MINISTER: Rise woman. You are this day blessed. Rise.

OLD WOMAN *(pushes herself up on her hands but continues to sing)*: Leaning, etc.

MINISTER: The Lord works in mysterious ways, my boy. Look at this woman beseiged with the spirit.

HOMOSEXUAL: An ambitious ecstasy.

BOY: Does she still think I am sent by the devil?

HOMOSEXUAL: And if so, why not? The devil is a part of creation like any ash tray or senator. Why segregate him?

MINISTER: The host of evil. You cannot even speak of him.

BOY: The devil is evil. He is Satan.

HOMOSEXUAL: A victim of ambition. They say that to us. Milton, with the bad ear. Dante, the Catholic, gives him no place. No portion of goodness or human shape. But Milton's bad poetry has it so. Satan threw down what was only subjection to become a king, unlike this old whore writhing on the floor, singing that old nigger song. Now, even our noble pastor cannot put that down. A king! Do you hear that you fraud.

OLD WOMAN *(singing still, waving her hand)*: The Light. The Light. Holy cock of creation.

HOMOSEXUAL: Oh, my Christ, what lousy taste. *(To BOY.)* Is that what you wanted from our dear Satan? Banality? Cock of creation. Bah. She takes flesh, just like you did son, but she makes it abstract and useless. So it is holy and harmless. I pee on her Jesus if he but dare to tell me who and when I can get laid. And your evil spirit. Hah. A man who made himself a ruler. If God is omnipotent, it is his doing, as well. And who killed all those Egyptians with all that water? Satan? Bullshit. That ignorant woman's lord in his wretched community of sterile eavesdroppers.

MINISTER: You blaspheme!

HOMOSEXUAL: Goddammit. Don't use that cornball expression again, will you? Let it be politics or shut up.

MINISTER: Fascist!

HOMOSEXUAL: Liberal!

OLD WOMAN (*moaning*): God!

BOY: Am I saved?

HOMOSEXUAL: Saved? From what? What would you be saved from?

BOY: From Satan.

MINISTER: And his hosts!

HOMOSEXUAL: And miss something? Not, not me. I want it all. I want nothing to pass me. I want to know it. See it. *(Smiles.)* Feel it, if it comes to that. Feel it here, in my fingers. *(Dances. Sings.)* The God. The God. The political God. Come commentators, salesmen, radicals, let no one say we have not tried to be everything. Let no one say we have not fucked everything and everyone we could. Let no one say we failed the spirit of the Renaissance. I be Giotto of the queers. I be Willie Mays of the queers. I not be lim-lim limited to tiny nigger songs. Dance with me, boy.

BOY: I cannot.

MINISTER: He must not. He can yet be saved.

HOMOSEXUAL: Can yet be made sterile. Can yet be taught that blank walls yodel the crazy name of salvation. Can yet see thunder in a straw. I make all my beds, and baby, I lie in them. *(Laughs.)*

Through the doors of the church—outer doors of the theater—singing is heard, then the doors are pushed open and a procession of WOMEN, *perhaps six, young girls, of diverse sizes and colors, wearing gauzy gowns with huge numbers pinned to their chests march slowly in, and down the aisle, singing. The singing is a chant, a slow steady dirge, with the medieval drum being beaten in the background. No, one carries the drum, and beats out the rhythm of the march. Some carry candles. Some carry trumpets, which they attempt from time to time to blow. No sound issues, except their singing and the drum.*

WOMEN: Jesus wants me for a sunbeam, a sunbeam, a sunbeam. Jesus wants me for a sunbeam, to shine for him, each day.

The OLD WOMAN *on the floor stops her singing for a moment in order to hear what the* WOMEN *are singing. Then she takes up their song, but rises from the floor and begins to do a slow off-time seductive dance, starting to take off more skirts.*

OLD WOMAN: Get it, ladies. Get it. *(Puts her hands behind her head and shakes her hips, and does little skips.)* Dance with me, boy.

BOY: Dance? You are a holy woman. A devout person. You know I can't dance with you.

OLD WOMAN: Dance with me, boy.

MINISTER: Have you gone mad? This is the Lord's house.

HOMOSEXUAL: Dance with me, boy.

MINISTER: Stop it. Stop it. This is the Lord's house.

BOY: I can't dance. This is the Lord's house. I've already sinned.

WOMEN *stop in front of dais. Singing quietly with their heads down.*

HOMOSEXUAL: Sinned? You mean because you whacked your doodle? How old are you?

BOY: Fifteen.

HOMOSEXUAL: How many times have you jerked off?

BOY: How many? Oh, father, I have not told you everything.

MINISTER: Everything?

BOY: Yes. That I've sinned each time I've prayed.

HOMOSEXUAL: How many prayers?

BOY: One after every meal.

HOMOSEXUAL: For how long?

BOY *(sobbing)*: For one year.

HOMOSEXUAL: Hmm. 365 days, 3 meals a day, that's one thousand ninety-five meat beatings. Not bad. Not bad.

MINISTER: My God!

HOMOSEXUAL: Oh, shut up you old hypocrite. I bet you topped that figure years running.

MINISTER: My God! The Lord will strike you dead.

HOMOSEXUAL: That's okay. It never happened before. It might be a gas. I mean drilled with the holy lightning and all that shit. Wow! *(Sings.)* Drill me baby. Drill me so I don't need to be drilled no more.

OLD WOMAN: A holy man!

BOY: What shall I do?

HOMOSEXUAL: Become a Christian so you can understand the symbolism. Cut the comedy.

MINISTER: Yes. Embrace the Holy Ghost. Let me baptize you.

BOY: Yes father. I want to be baptized. I want to see God.

OLD WOMAN: A true Christian believer!

HOMOSEXUAL: Hey, that might not be such a bad idea. Yea! See the cat, finally.

MINISTER: Are you all of one mind?

HOMOSEXUAL: You might say that. *(Notices* **WOMEN.***)* Hey, why don't you bitches shut the fuck up. *(Chorus soft hum. Gestures with head in their direction.)* Hey, padre, who're these paraplegics?

MINISTER: The hosts of the Lord. The virgins of Christ's love. My usherettes.

HOMOSEXUAL: Flies! Harpies! Working girls! Go back to your apartments and wait for a phone call. Go to the bar and read a paperback. But don't try to queer my, ahem, scene.

MINISTER: How dare you?

HOMOSEXUAL: How dare I not? Tell me something inspiring about these beatniks and perhaps I'll relent.

MINISTER: They have all been embraced by the Lord's light. Brides of the Lord's son, our own Jesus Christ.

BOY *(strangely agitated)*: I must be baptized!

MINISTER: You will. You will, my son. I will prepare you.

HOMOSEXUAL: Out, ladies! *(Shooing them.)* Out! Go home and pin up some Picasso prints or something.

WOMEN *(raise their heads and begin singing again loudly)*: Yes, Jesus loves me. Yes, Jesus love me. Yes, Jesus love me, cause the Bible tells me so.

HOMOSEXUAL: You will never be interesting.

OLD WOMAN: They are the hosts of the Lord, the wives of His son.

HOMOSEXUAL: They also have extremely bad taste. Go home to your wretched Electra complexes.

BOY: Father, I must be baptized! I feel the sin returning. That hardness in my flesh.

WOMEN *(first one looks up)*: That boy! He's the one. *(All join in.)* That boy!

BOY: Oh!

WOMEN: The Christ child come back. He is the Son of God. Our Lord Jesus Christ. Chief Religious jelly roll of the universe.

BOY: Oh!

MINISTER: What do they mean, son?

All their speeches are staggered among them by sentence or phrase.

WOMEN: He is the Son of Man. The big stroker of the universe. It was he who popped us. *(They all moan ecstatically, sinking to their knees, praying.)* God bless mommy and daddy, and Rochester, and Uncle Don. And please God bring me a new baby sister.

BOY: Oh!

MINISTER: What do they mean?

WOMEN: He is the Son of God. Our holy husband. It was he who popped us in those various hallways of love and blessed us with the beauty of Jehovah. *(Some of the WOMEN are still praying.)* And bring me a new doll, and a monopoly set, and an FM radio and a picture of Monk. . .

MINISTER *(sinks to his knees)*: You? The Christ? The Messiah? The holy husband?

OLD WOMAN *(sinks to her knees)*: Christ. Christ. Jesus.

HOMOSEXUAL *(looking at him sideways)*: Yeh? Well, that's a wig. Prove it!

BOY: Oh!

MINISTER *(kissing the Boy's feet)*: Oh, Jesus bless me, I beg of you.

OLD WOMAN: Yes, Jesus. Bless us. Please, bless us. We are only useless human flesh, but we love your word and have placed our lives in your service.

HOMOSEXUAL: Do something. Lemme see you turn this place into the White House or something cool like that.

BOY *(also sinking to his knees)*: Oh, father, please please forgive me. I'm not the Christ. That is also part of my sin. I'm only an ignorant boy who's whacked it off over a thousand times this year. I lied to the girls.

WOMEN *(they are swooning on their knees, writhing in ecstasy)*: Beautiful screw of the universe!

MINISTER: Jesus.

BOY: Father, I'm not the Christ. I lied. I am only flesh.

HOMOSEXUAL: Let's see.

BOY: See my hands. *(Holds up his palms.)* There are no holes, no rents in my flesh. I am a whole and ignorant youth. I thought I might save the girls by telling them I was related to God. I didn't say Son. They only assumed.

HOMOSEXUAL: Very tricky. Yeh. Very tricky. *(Pats **BOY** on shoulders.)* I might try that idea myself. Yeh. Related. Hah. *(Muses.)* Only my friends are so much more sophisticated than yours.

OLD WOMAN: Son of God. Bless us.

MINISTER: Yes, Christ, make us whole. Deliver us from our miseries.

HOMOSEXUAL: Hey. Hey. Why don't you dopes get up? You heard what the kid said. It's all a joke. He just put these art majors in a trick. Get up. Take a look at genius.

BOY: Yes father, I lied! I've sinned. Please get up. Forgive me. Father, I lied.

MINISTER: Lied? You mean you're not the Christ? Another false alarm. First, Simon Magnus, then Garvey, now you. God damn! You mean you lied merely to further your lust.

HOMOSEXUAL: Why else?

BOY *(weeping)*: Yes. Yes, father. Please forgive me. Please.

OLD WOMAN: Lied? *(Screams.)* Blasphemer! You are the devil. Satan! You are the blackest evil.

WOMEN: Ohh. Christ. Fucked for nothing. We wanted to be virgins of the Lord. He lied. He lied. Ohhh.

MINISTER: You are a sinner. That was the sin of the Leopard. Evil youth you are truly damned.

HOMOSEXUAL: Oh, don't ham everything up!

BOY: Oh, father, forgive me.

OLD WOMAN: Blasphemer. You spilled your seed in prayer. You sacrificed these blessed vestals to your lust. You should die! Die!

MINISTER: May the true God strike you dead.

WOMEN: May our true husband-to-be castrate you with his lightning. Liar! Devil!

The MINISTER, OLD WOMAN *and the six girls move toward the* BOY *wailing.*

ALL: Evil. Evil. Sinner. Son of Satan. Blasphemer.

HOMOSEXUAL: Quiet, you obnoxious mediocrities! I say, be quiet.

BOY: Father, have you no charity? Forgive me. It was the mistake of youth. Forgive me, blessed vestals. Forgive me, devout mother. I have made no sacrilege except to yield to the boomings of my flesh. I am not, not, evil. *(Weeps.)* Father. *(Looks toward heaven.)* Why have you forsaken me? Again?

MINISTER: Blasphemy, still?

OLD WOMAN: Old Nick. Evil spirit. We will kill you.

They all move toward the BOY *menacingly.*

HOMOSEXUAL: Fools! Assholes! Devout Citizens! Stop it! Go home to your radios!

They throw the HOMOSEXUAL *out of the way, kicking him as he falls.*

ALL: It is your sin!

MINISTER: You must be sacrificed to cleanse the soul of man. As the true Christ died for man. So you must die so that He should not have died for nothing. You must be sacrificed.

WOMEN: Sacrificed! Sacrificed! *(They sing.)* Leaning, leaning safe and secure from sin or harm. . .

The MINISTER *and* OLD WOMAN *are also singing.*

Leaning on the everlasting light.

They move dreadfully toward the BOY. *The* WOMEN *beat their drum.*

Blaspheme. Blaspheme! There must be a sacrifice.

MINISTER: We must cleanse ourselves.

OLD WOMAN: We must be clean.

WOMEN: We must be worthy of the true Messiah.

BOY *(at the* MINISTER*)*: Father, please forgive me. *(At the ceiling.)* Father, why have you forsaken me. Forgive me. I am only youth. Not sin or evil. Only youth. I ask forgiveness for your sins as well as my own.

MINISTER: You have sinned. We will cleanse ourselves.

OLD WOMAN: You must be sacrificed.

BOY: You would kill me?

MINISTER: We must.

WOMEN: We must be worthy.

BOY *(picks up his bag)*: You have no charity! No humanity. No love. *(Pulls long silver sword out of bag.)* No sense of your selves. It is not right that youth should die to cleanse your stinking hearts! I *am* the Son of God. The Christ. *(Begins to strike his attackers down with the sword.)* No charity! No love!

They fall screaming around him.

There will be no second crucifixion!

The MESSENGER *enters. He is a tall, gaunt man in a motor- cyclist's outfit, i.e., leather jacket and pants. Wheels his motorcycle into the church. Takes off his long leather gloves. He has a gold crown stenciled on the back of his jacket. Under the crown, the words: "The Man."*

MESSENGER: Hey. You.

BOY: Yes?

MESSENGER: What's happening?

BOY: I have slain these sinners. They had no charity.

MESSENGER: Oh? No charity, huh? *(Looks over the scene. Takes out notebook.)* Yeh. Who's this guy in the red tights?

BOY: They killed him. He tried to defend me. I am the Son of Man. The Christ.

MESSENGER: Yeh, I know. I came to get you. *(Starts a mambo step, which continues through most of the scene.)*

BOY: Came to get me?

MESSENGER: Yeh. The man sent me.

29

BOY: The man?

MESSENGER: Yeh. The man. Your father.

BOY: Oh? *(Looks at the* MESSENGER.*)* Oh, I recognize you. You're one of the messengers.

MESSENGER: Yeh. I'm closing up this whole deal. The man don't like none of the action. It's all finished.

BOY: But he sent me here to save them. This earth.

MESSENGER: Yeh, I know. But you been fuckin' up royally. You agree?

BOY: Agree? No. I don't agree. I have brought love to many people.

MESSENGER: Well, it's not my doing. The man says you just blew your gig.

BOY: That's not true.

MESSENGER: I don't have time to argue, Percy, orders is orders. The man's destroying the whole works tonight. With a grenade.

BOY: What? Damn it. It's not fair. It's not fair. He didn't give me a chance.

MESSENGER: Chance? To do what? Murder some more people? Percy, baby, I got orders. Don't give me a hard time, please.

BOY: He's not going to destroy this place. I won't let him. And I'm not going anyplace with you.

MESSENGER: Oh, now come on Percy, will you. *(Looks at his watch.)* It's twelve now. The man's going to start the fireworks as soon as the bars let out. Only three more hours. *(Does tricky mambo step.)* Hooo!

BOY: No. No. *(Kneels in supplication.)* Father. Father. *(Looking toward ceiling.)* Don't give up on me. You have no charity.

MESSENGER: Oh, man.

BOY: Have compassion for them, father. Have compassion for me.

MESSENGER: Hoooo! *(Springs.)*

BOY: Father! Compassion!

MESSENGER *(looks at watch)*: O.K. Percy, let's roll. I got miles to go before I sleep.

BOY: No! I will stay here on earth, and perish with them. If their sin is my doing, then I will suffer with them. Leave me!

MESSENGER: Sorry, baby. Can't make it. I gotta job to do just like everybody else. Jump on the back of the cycle and we'll split.

BOY: No! I refuse. Neither God nor man shall force me to leave. I was sent here to save man and I'll not leave until I do. Nothing will make me forsake this flesh. *(Screams at ceiling.)* I will not leave!

MESSENGER: Aw, Percy, goddamn. *(Walks over and hits him over the head with a tire iron.)* This kid's always been a drag. *(Hoists Boy's body onto his shoulder, puts him on the back of the motorcycle, does one more mambo step, then wheels the cycle out. Its engines are heard turning over off-stage.)*

The light is dimming slightly, perhaps from white to blue. From the pile of bodies, the **HOMOSEXUAL** *manages to extricate himself. He shakes his head, then rises slowly to the center.*

HOMOSEXUAL: Good Christ, what's happened in this place? *(Turns Minister's body over with his toe.)* Serves him right for catering to rough trade. All out like lights. I better get out of here before somebody comes in and asks me to help clean the place up. Damn, looks like some really uninteresting kind of orgy went on in here. *(Looks at watch.)* Hmmmmm. 1:30. I got about an hour before the bars close. Think I'll drift on up to 42nd Street and cruise Bickford's. *(Starts to leave.)* Wonder what happened to that cute little religious fanatic? *(Does his ballet step. Starts to sing his song.)* God, Go-od, God, etc.

BLACK

THE TOILET

The Toilet was first presented by Leo Garen and Stan Swerdlow at the St. Marks Playhouse, New York, on December 16, 1964. It was directed by Leo Garen, designed by Larry Rivers, and the lighting was by Harold Baldridge. The cast was as follows:

ORA .... James Spruill

WILLIE LOVE .... Gary Bolling

HINES .... D'Urville Martin

JOHNNY BOY HOLMES .... Bostic Van Felton

PERRY .... Norman Bush

GEORGE DAVIS .... Antonio Fargas

SKIPPY .... Tony Hudson

KNOWLES .... Walter Jones

DONALD FARRELL .... Gary Haynes

FOOTS .... Hampton Clanton

KAROLIS .... Jaime Sanchez

CHARACTERS

ORA (Big Shot): *Short, ugly, crude, loud.*

WILLIE LOVE: *Tall, thin. Should have been sensitive. Smiles.*

HINES: *Big, husky, garrulous. He and Love are closest friends.*

JOHNNY BOY HOLMES: *Short, curly hair. Bright, fast, likable.*

PERRY: *Tall, dark, somber, cynical.*

GEORGE DAVIS: *Tall, thin, crudely elegant. Judicious.*

SKIPPY: *Quick. Rather stupid but interested. Someone to be trusted.*

KNOWLES: *Large and ridiculous. A grinning ape.*

DONALD FARRELL: *Tall, thin, blonde, awkward, soft.*

FOOTS (Ray): *Short, intelligent, manic. Possessor of a threatened empire.*

KAROLIS: *Medium height. Very skinny and not essentially attractive except when he speaks.*

The scene is a large bare toilet built of gray rough cement. There are urinals along one wall and a partition separating them from the commodes which are along the same wall. The toilet must resemble the impersonal ugliness of a school toilet or a latrine of some institution. A few rolls of toilet paper are spread out on the floor, wet through. The actors should give the impression frequently that the place smells.

Ora breaks through the door grinning, then giggling. Looks around the bleak place, walks around, then with one hand on his hip takes out his joint and pees, still grinning, into one of the commodes, spraying urine over the seat.

LOVE *(sticking his head through the door)*: Big Shot! Hey, Big Shot! These guys say come and help them.

ORA *(zipping his fly and wiping the one hand on the back of his pants)*: Yeh? *(Turning to LOVE.)* Yeh? They got him, huh?

LOVE *(pushing door open so his arm is straight)*: Naw, they don't have him yet. He's on the second floor, running back and forth and hiding in empty rooms. But Knowles said for you to come help.

ORA *(flushing all the commodes and urinals in the row as he walks past)*: Sheet! I'll catch that bastid in a second. *(Ducks under Love's arm to go out.)* Why the hell don't you get up there. You supposed to be faster than me.

LOVE: I'm s'posed to stay here and keep the place clear. *(Making a face.)* Damn. This place smells like hell.

ORA *(without turning around)*: Yeh *(giggling)*, this must be your momma's house.

37

LOVE *(slipping inside the door and holding it against* **ORA***):* Shit. At least I got one.

ORA *(thumps against the door, not really angry):* Bastid!

LOVE *waits a few seconds, then pulls the door open slightly. Then lets it shut and walks to a closed commode and noticing it's wet wipes it with some of the strewn toilet paper. He sits down and stretches his legs. Then gets up and opens the commode to pee. There are voices outside and then the door swings open and* **HINES** *and* **HOLMES** *come in.*

HINES: Hey, Willie.

LOVE *(still peeing):* What you want? *(Comes out, zipping his pants.)*

HINES *(to* **HOLMES***):* Man, this cat's in here pulling his whatchamacallit.

HOLMES *(to* **LOVE***):* Yeh. Damn, Love, why don't you go get Gloria to do that stuff for you.

LOVE: She-et. *(Grinning.)* Huh. I sure don't need your ol' lady to be pullin' on my joint. *(Laughs.* **HOLMES** *begins to spar with him.)*

HINES: They didn't even catch that skinny nose punk yet.

LOVE: No? Why in hell not?

HOLMES: He's still running up and down the damn halls. I should go up there and drag that sonofabitch down.

HOLMES *and* **HINES** *begin to pee also in the commodes.*

LOVE *pulls open the door a small bit and looks out.*

LOVE: Shit. Boy, all you slow ass cats. I'd catch that little skinny paddy boy in a second. Where's that little popeyed Foots?

HINES: Damn if I know. I think he's still in Miss Powell's class. You know if he missed her class she'd beat his head, and then get his ol' lady to beat his head again.

HOLMES: Shit. Skippy should've got hold of that damn Karolis by now. He ain't fast worth a bitch.

LOVE: Yeh, but he's so goddamned scary he might just jump out a goddamn window.

HOLMES *finishes peeing and starts pushing* LOVE *and they begin to spar around.* HOLMES *is very funny, making boxer-like sounds and brushing his nose continuously with his thumbs.* LOVE *just stands straight with his left hand stiff and stabbing it out toward Holmes' face.* HINES *finishes and gets in the action too. Both he and* HOLMES *are against* LOVE, *who starts to laugh and curse good naturedly.*

LOVE: Two a' you bastids, huh? I'll take you both. *(He starts kicking at them.)*

HINES: Boy, if you kick me, you'll die just like that. . .with your skinny ass leg up. They'll have to build you a special coffin with a part for your leg.

HOLMES *(backing away, and then turning on* HINES. *Laughing):* Let's get this sum'bitch, Willie.

HINES *(backing away, now kicking and swinging. . .but just tim-*

ing blows so they won't strike anyone): Goddamn, Johnny Boy, you a crooked muthafucka. You cats think you can mess with the kid?

The two spar against HINES *and then* LOVE *turns against* HOLMES.

LOVE: Let's get this little assed cat.

HOLMES *kicks at them, then jumps up on the commodes in order to defend himself more "heroically."*

HOLMES: I'm gonna get your ass, Willie. I'm just trying to help you out and you gonna play wise. Ya' bastid.

HINES: Listen to that cat. (*Runs after* HOLMES.) I'm gonna put your damn head in one of those damn urinals.

He and LOVE *finally grab* HOLMES *and he begins struggling with them in earnest.*

Let's put this little bastard's head in the goddamn urinal!

HOLMES: You bastids! Let me go! I'm gonna cut somebody. Bastids!

The door opens and ORA *comes in. His shirt is torn. But he rushes over laughing and starts punching everyone, even* HOLMES.

HINES: Goddamn it, Big Shot, get the hell out of here.

HOLMES: Get 'em, Big Shot.

ORA (*punches* HOLMES *who's still being held by* LOVE): I'm gonna punch you, you prick. Hold the cocksucker, Love.

LOVE *(releasing* HOLMES *immediately):* I ain't gonna hold him so you can punch him.

ORA *and* HOLMES *square off, both laughing and faking professional demeanor.*

LOVE: Hey, Big Shot, what happened to your shirt?

ORA *(putting his hands down and handling the torn part of his shirt):* That muthafuckin' Karolis ripped it.

The other three yowl. HINES *puts his fingers to the hole as if to tear it again.*

Get outta here you black ass bastid. *(He squares off at* HINES, *then pushes him away.)* That paddy bastid! I had the cocksucker around the waist, and then he rips my shirt and scratches me. *(He holds up his wounded hand.)*

HINES: You let him get away?

ORA: No, hell. I punched the bastid right in his lip. But he was making so much noise we thought somebody'd come out and see us so Knowles and Skippy took him in the broom closet and I cut down the stairs. The stupid bastid was screaming and biting right outside of ol' lady Powell's room.

HOLMES: Did anybody come outta there?

ORA: You think I was gonna stay around and see? She and Miss Golden after me anyway.

LOVE: Did you see Foots in there?

ORA *(going to the door and peering out)*: Yeh. And George Davis and Perry are in there too. *(He pushes door open and leans all the way out.)*

HINES: Shit. They're never gonna bring that sonofabitch down here. We ain't got all day.

ORA *(letting the door shut)*: Yeh, Perry and Foots and them ought to be down here in a few minutes. It's almost 3:00 now.

LOVE *(pretending he has a basketball in his hands, he pretends to dribble and lunges forward simulating a fake at **HINES**, then he sweeps past **HINES** and leaps in the air as if making a layup shot)*: Peed on you, just then, buddy.

HINES: Sheet, Man, you what you call a self-checker. I don't even have to block that shot. I just take it off the backboard like this. *(He spins around and leaps up at the imaginary basket and scoops the imaginary ball off, landing and shaking his head as if to shake off imaginary defenders.)* Another rebound! *(Makes motion of long pass down toward opposite "court.")* Now, the fast break *(He moves in position for his own pass, receives it, makes one long stepping dribble and leaps as if dunking the ball in the basket.)* Two!

HOLMES: Boy, you guys sure play a lot of ball. . .off the court.

ORA *(opening the door again)*: No Shootin' cocksuckas.

LOVE *(still whirling and leaping as if he is making successful hook shots from an imaginary foul line)*: Hey, what we gonna do to this cat when he gets here?

ORA *(leaning back in from the door though keeping it open with his fingers)*: Damn, Love. You a stupid bastid. *(Peeks out door.)* We gonna kick that little frail bastid's ass.

HINES: In fact, you the one gonna do it, Willie.

HOLMES: Yeh, Love. *(Blocking one of Love's "shots.")*

LOVE: Shit. Karolis never bothered me. *(Faking **HOLMES** and swinging to shoot from the other side.)*

ORA *(looking back in and letting the door swing shut)*: Damn, Willie *(in mocking seriousness)*, Karolis is always telling everybody how he bangs the hell out of Caroline, every chance he gets. *(Begins to giggle.)*

HOLMES: Is that your mother's name, Love, Caroline?

HINES *(busy trying to lift a back window to look out on the yard)*: What you mean, Johnny Boy, is that his mother's name? You the one told me.

LOVE *(swinging around as if to shoot again he suddenly punches **HOLMES** on the shoulder. **HOLMES** lets out a yelp of pain)*: Uhhuh. . .I told you about messin' with me.

HOLMES *(holding his shoulder)*: Shit. Why didn't you hit Big Shot, you bastard? He brought the shit up.

ORA *(has the door propped open again)*: Shit. That narrow head bastid know better than to fuck with me. *(He peers out the door and as he does **LOVE** gestures as if to hit him in the back.)*

43

HOLMES *(to LOVE)*: You scared ass bastard. Why don't you do it?

ORA *(turning around and throwing up his hands to defend himself)*: Yeh, I wish you would, you bullet head sonofabitch.

HOLMES *goes and sits on a radiator next to HINES.*

LOVE: Man, nobody's thinking about you, Big Shot. *(He goes to pee.)*

ORA *(pulling the door open again)*: Here come Perry and them.

HOLMES *(jumping off the radiator still holding his shoulder)*: Perry and who else?

ORA: George Davis and Donald Farrell.

HINES: Donald Farrell? What the hell's he doin' down here? Where the hell is Foots?

LOVE: Yeh, what the hell is Perry doing bringing Farrell down here with 'em? Shit.

ORA *pulls the door open, and PERRY, DAVIS and FARRELL come in.*

PERRY: Hey, what's happening?

HOLMES: Shit. I should ask you. Where's Foots?

GEORGE: He had to stay upstairs for awhile. Powell wanted to talk to him. . .or something.

ORA *(to FARRELL)*: Man, whatta you want down here? Nobody

asked you to come.

GEORGE: I told him he could come. Why not?

ORA: Whatta you mean, why not? You know goddamn well, why not. Silly sumbitch!

PERRY: Ah, Big Shot, why don't you be cool for a change, huh?

GEORGE: Yeh, man, Big Shot. Donald's not going to hurt anything.

ORA: No? *(Taking out a much-smoked cigarette butt.)* Maybe you don't think so. . .but I do.

GEORGE: Oh, man, shit.

FARRELL: Why don't you want me here, Big Shot?

ORA *(glaring at* FARRELL*)*: Man, don't be asking me questions.

FARRELL: Don't ask you questions? Why the hell not?

ORA *(menacingly at* FARRELL*)*: Cause I said so, that's why You don't like it, muthafucka?

PERRY *(stepping between them)*: Goddamn it, Big Shot, why don't you sit your ass down for awhile and shut the hell up?

ORA *(turning to* PERRY*)*: You gonna make me, muthafucka?

PERRY *(stepping to face* ORA*)*: I can. And you better believe it, Baby!

ORA: Shit. *(Disparagingly. Moving away from* FARRELL *and*

45

back to the center of the room.) Well you damn sure got your chance right now, you black sonofabitch.

GEORGE *(moves between* PERRY *and* ORA*)*: Oh, goddamnit why don't both you guys sit down. You too, Donald.

FARRELL *moves to sit on a radiator beside* HOLMES *and* HINES.

Ora, you wrong, man, and you know it.

ORA: How come I'm wrong, huh? You know goddamn well that skinny cocksucka over there *(at* FARRELL*)* ain't got no business down here. He ain't gonna do a damn thing but stand around and look.

LOVE *(laughing)*: That's all I'm gonna do.

HINES *(hunching* HOLMES *with his elbow)*: Yeh, but that's okay for you, Willie. You so black, if you stand still nobody'll know you're standing there anyway.

All laugh. ORA *takes the opportunity to go to the door and crack it open.*

PERRY: Where's the rest of those guys?

HINES: I guess they must still be upstairs in that broom closet.

PERRY: Broom closet?

He and DAVIS *lean against one of the walls and begin to smoke.*

HINES: Yeh, Knowles and Skippy got Karolis upstairs in a

broom closet waiting till everybody leaves the floor I guess.

FARRELL: Jimmy Karolis?

HOLMES: Yeah, that's who we're waiting for. *(Giggles.)*

FARRELL: What the hell's gonna happen then?

ORA *(turning from door)*: Man, what the hell you care, huh? Pee-the-bed-muthafucka!

HINES: Damn, George!

GEORGE: Damn, what?

HINES: Seems to me like Big Shot's right. You bring this cat down here and he doesn't even know what's happening.

ORA: You goddamn real I'm right. Simple ass cats.

FARRELL: What're you guys gonna gang Jimmy Karolis?

ORA: We gonna break that muthafucka's back.

FARRELL: For what?

ORA: Look man, why don't you shut up and get the hell out of here, huh?

FARRELL: You mean all you guys're gonna jump on Karolis?

ORA *(walking over to* FARRELL *and grabbing him by the shirt)*: You gonna stick up for him?

FARRELL *tries to push Ora's hands from his shirt, and*

though he is much taller than **ORA,** **ORA** *pulls him from his seat.*

FARRELL: Goddamn it, Ora, why don't you cut the shit?

GEORGE: Yeh, Ora, cut it out.

PERRY: Goddamn; that cat's always going for bad.

GEORGE *comes over to restrain* **ORA,** *but* **ORA** *succeeds in punching* **FARRELL** *in the stomach.* **FARRELL** *clutches his stomach and sinks to the floor groaning.*

PERRY: *(to* **ORA***):* You bastard.

ORA *swings around to confront him.*

ORA: You come on too, if you want to, you black sonofabitch!

GEORGE *pushes them apart again and his push sends* **ORA** *rattling heavily against the door.*

Goddamnit, George, why don't you stay the fuck out of this?

GEORGE: Because there wasn't a goddamn reason in the world for you to hit Donald like that. *(Going to help* **FARRELL** *up.)* Damn, Ora, you're a wrong sonofabitch, you know that?

FARRELL *(still doubled up and holding his stomach. He pulls his arm back when* **GEORGE** *tries to help him up):* No, man! Lemme stay here. *(Still groaning.)* Ora, you dirty cocksucker.

ORA: Boy, you better shut up before I stomp mudholes in your pissy ass.

The door is suddenly pushed open and **KNOWLES** *and* **SKIPPY** *come in holding* **KAROLIS** *by the arms. Karolis' head is hanging, and he is crying softly and blood is on his shirt and face. His hair is mussed and standing all over his head.*

LOVE: Ga-uh damn! What'd you cats do?

KNOWLES *(giggling stupidly)*: Love, now what the hell does it look like we did? Broke this muthafucka's jaw.

HINES: Damn. I thought we were just bringing the cat down here to fight Foots. I didn't know you guys were gonna break his head first.

SKIPPY: Well, he didn't wanna come. We had to persuade him.

KNOWLES: Shit, Skippy, whatta you mean "we?" I did all the persuading.

ORA: Aw, shit, Knowles. I bloodied the cat's lip. You trying to take all the credit.

SKIPPY: Yeh, Knowles. You didn't hit the cat but once, and that was on the goddamn shoulder.

Letting **KNOWLES** *drag* **KAROLIS** *into a corner where he lets him drop.*

You know what this cat was doing all the time we was in that goddamn broom closet? Tellin' jokes. *(Laughs.)* They must not a been funny either. Karolis didn't laugh once.

KNOWLES: What should I do with this guy. I gotta drag him everywhere.

ORA: Drop him in that goddamn corner. *(Walks over to corner and nudges KAROLIS with his foot.)* Hey, muthafucka. Hey! Why don't you straighten up?

SKIPPY *(noticing FARRELL, who is still crumpled in an opposite corner, but stirring)*: Damn! What the hell happened to Donald?

PERRY: That goddamn Big Shot had to show how bad he was.

ORA *(laughing paradoxically)*: He called me a nigger.

All laugh.

LOVE: Well, what the hell are you? Wha's the matter, you shamed of your people?

ORA: Fuck you! *(He still stands over KAROLIS, nudging him with 'his foot.)* Hey, man, get up! *(Laughs.)*

HINES: Damn, Ora. Why don't you leave the cat alone?

ORA *(bending over as if to talk in KAROLIS' ear)*: Hey, baby, why don't you get up? I gotta nice fat sausage here for you.

GEORGE: Goddamn, Big Shot. . .You really a wrong sonofabitch!

ORA: Look man. *(Now kneeling over the slumped figure.)* If you want to get in on this you line up behind me. I don't give a shit what you got to say.

LOVE: Man, George, leave the cat alone. You know that's his stick. That's what he does *(laughing)* for his kicks. . .rub up against half-dead white boys.

All laugh.

ORA (*looking over his shoulder. . .grudgingly having to smile too*): I'd rub up against your momma too. (*Leaning back to* KAROLIS.) Come on, baby. . .I got this fat ass sa-zeech for you!

LOVE: Ora, you mad cause you don't have a momma of your own to rub up against.

All laugh.

ORA (*turns again, this time less amused*): Fuck you, you bony head sonofabitch. As long as I can rub against your momma . . .or your fatha' (*laughs at his invention*) I'm doin' alright.

Door is pushed open suddenly and FOOTS *comes in. He is nervous but keeps it hidden by a natural glibness and a sharp sense of what each boy in the room expects, singularly, from him. He is the weakest physically and smallest of the bunch, but he is undoubtedly their leader. When* FOOTS *comes in* KAROLIS *looks up quickly, then slumps again.*

HINES: Man, where the hell you been?

FOOTS: That goddamn Van Ness had me in his office. He said I'm a credit to my race. (*Laughs and all follow.*) He said I'm smart-as-a-whip (*imitating Van Ness*) and should help him to keep all you unsavory (*again imitating*) elements in line.

All laugh again.

LOVE: Yeh? What's he talking about?

FOOTS: Well, he seems to think that you guys. . .particularly that goddamn Big Shot and Knowles, are not good influences in this joint.

PERRY: Boy, you can say that again. Nutty muthafuckas!

ORA *(to PERRY)*: Fuck you, tar baby!

FOOTS: Well, I'm supposed to make sure that you guys don't do anything bad to anybody. Especially to James Karolis. *(Laughing.)*

GEORGE: Oh yeh? He know about that?

FOOTS: Yeh, somebody told him Knowles said he was gonna kick Karolis' ass. *(Seeing* **KAROLIS** *in the corner for the first time. His first reaction is horror and disgust. . .but he keeps it controlled as is his style, and merely half-whistles.)* Goddamn! What the fuck happened to him? *(He goes over to* **KAROLIS** *and kneels near him, threatening to stay too long. He controls the impulse and gets up and walks back to where he was. He is talking throughout his action.)* Damn! What'd you guys do, kill the cat?

PERRY: Heavy handed Big Shot again.

FOOTS *(looks at* ORA *quickly with disgust but softens it immediately to comic disdain)*: What the hell you hit him with, Ora, a goddamn train?

ORA *(happy at the notice of his destruction)*: No, man, I just bopped him in the mouth with the back of my hand.

FOOTS: Ga-uhd damn! You a rough ass cat, Shot. He sure don't look like he's in any way to fight anybody.

ORA *(laughing)*: No, but he might be able to suck you off. Hee, hee.

LOVE: Shit. You the one that look like you want that, Big Shot.

FOOTS: Oh, shit. There wasn't any need of bringing the cat down here if you guys were gonna fuck him up before I got here. He was supposed to fight me. *(Almost angry.)*

HINES: Yeh, that's what I thought. You shouldn't of sent Ora and Knowles up after him then.

FOOTS: The only person I asked to go up was Skippy.

SKIPPY: Well, the sonofabitch wouldn't come. . .so, I got Super-duck over there to help me. I didn't ask Ora to come. Knowles did.

KNOWLES: Oh, man, the cat's here. Get him up on his feet *(laughs)* then knock him down. That's all. That don't seem like no big problem to me. *(Through most of the action KNOWLES is drumming on the walls or the window or the door or the floor, in a kind of drum and bugle corps beat. . .also supplying the bugle parts vocally.)*

LOVE: Man, Knowles, why don't you stop being a goddamn Elk all the time. Damn. That cat's always drumming on something. Why don't you get a goddamn drum?

KNOWLES: I'm going to drum on your bony head in a little while if you don't shut up.

FOOTS: Well, I don't see any reason to keep all this shit up. Just pour water on the cat and let's get outta here.

ORA: What? You mean you made us go through all this bullshit for nothing?

FOOTS: Well, what the hell am I gonna do, beat on the guy while he's sprawled on the floor. Damn, Ora, you're a pretty lousy sonofabitch.

HINES: Man, Big Shot'd stomp anybody in any damn condition. He likes it when they're knocked out first, especially.

FOOTS: I'm pushed! There's no reason to stay here. I can't fight the guy like he is.

FARRELL *(who has pushed himself up and is leaning against the wall)*: I sure am glad somebody's got some sense here.

FOOTS *(seeing* **FARRELL** *for the first time)*: What the hell you doing here? Who asked you to come here, huh? *(Embarrassed and angry.)*

ORA: That stupid ass Perry brought him.

PERRY: That's right. I just thought there was gonna be a fight. I didn't know you guys were gonna lynch anybody.

FOOTS: Lynch, your ass. Look, Donald, why don't you leave, huh? Nobody needs you here.

FARRELL *(slowly)*: Yeh, okay, Ray. But I just want to know why you're gonna beat up on Jimmy like this. What the hell did he do to you?

FOOTS *(almost indignantly)*: None of your goddamn business, Farrell. Just leave!

ORA: Yeh, man. I should've thrown your ass out when you first come in here. Pee-the-bed sonofabitch.

FARRELL: O.K. *(Stands up, still lightly holding his stomach.)*

O.K. But I want to take Jimmy out of here with me. He can't fight anybody.

ORA: Man, you better shut your goddamn mouth and get outta here!

FOOTS: Look, Donald, just leave, that's all. You hear? *(Turns his back on* FARRELL *and walks toward* KAROLIS, *then thinking better of it turns toward* FARRELL *again.)*

FARRELL: Ray! You're not gonna beat the guy up when he's like that are you?

FOOTS: I don't need you to tell me what to do. *(He goes over and pulls the door open slightly.)* Just get out of here. . .now!

FARRELL *(takes a step then looks toward* KAROLIS*)*: But look at him, he can't do anything. *(To* FOOTS.*)* Why do you want to do this?

FOOTS: Goddamn it, get out!

FARRELL: That's no answer.

FOOTS: Man, I'll punch you in the belly myself.

FARRELL: Shit. *(Disparagingly. . .which makes* FOOTS *madder.)*

FOOTS *(in low horrible voice)*: Goddamnit. You better get the fuck outta here, right now!

FARRELL: Nobody's gonna tell me why? *(He starts to move for the door.)*

PERRY: Look, Donald, you better cool it, Buddy. You heard about that letter didn't you?

FARRELL: Letter? What letter?

FOOTS: Man, I told you to leave. I'm not gonna tell you again.

PERRY (*laughing*): The letter Karolis sent Foots telling him he thought he was "beautiful". . .and that he wanted to blow him.

All giggle.

FARRELL (*turning sharply toward* FOOTS): A letter?

ORA (*rushing at* FARRELL *from the side and punching him*): Goddamn it! Didn't you hear somebody say leave, pee ass?

FOOTS (*pushing between* FARRELL *and* ORA): Cut it out, Ora!

FARRELL (*hurt again and slumping.* ORA *tries to hit him again and the punch is blocked by* FOOTS *who glares savagely at* ORA): A letter? (*Groaning.*) Oh, Ray, come on. Why don't you come off it? (*He is looking up at* FOOTS.)

ORA (*leaps around* FOOTS *and pushes* FARRELL *into the door*): Get out of here you dumb bastid!

KNOWLES *pulls the door open and shoves* FARRELL *through it.*

Goddamn, what a stupid punk. (*He laughs, as do some of the others.*)

FOOTS (*stares at the closed door for a second, then he turns slowly to the others*): Look, let's get out of here. This stuff is finished.

KAROLIS *(has brought his head up during the preceding scuffle, and has been staring at* **FOOTS***. As* **FOOTS** *and the others look over toward him, he speaks very softly, but firmly)*: No. Nobody has to leave. I'll fight you, Ray. *(He begins to pull himself up. He is unsteady on his feet, but determined to get up. . .and to fight.)* I *want* to fight you.

FOOTS *is startled and his eyes widen momentarily, but he suppresses it.*

HINES: Damn. Some guys don't know when they're well off.

ORA: Yeh. You little skinny muthafucka. You should've kept your mouth shut, and played dead.

KNOWLES: Goddamn. You mean that sonofabitch wasn' dead? Shit, Big Shot, you must hit like a girl.

ORA *(to* **KNOWLES***)*: Yeh? Well, let me hit you, you bastid.

KNOWLES *(disparagingly)*: Shit.

KAROLIS *(pushing himself off the wall slightly and wiping his face with his sleeve)*: No, Ray. Don't have them leave. I want to fight you.

FOOTS *(very silent and stiff, not wanting to be pushed)*: Oh? *(Slowly.)* Well, that's damn fine with me.

ORA *(going behind* **KAROLIS** *and pushing him toward* **FOOTS***)*: You wanna fight? Well, go ahead, dick licker. *(Howls.)*

HINES: Yeh, get it on, fellas.

HOLMES: Karolis must be bad. *(Laughs.)*

GEORGE: Man *(to* KAROLIS*)* you sure you want to get in this? You look kinda shaky to me.

SKIPPY: Man, just sit down and watch. This might be good.

KAROLIS: Yes, Ray, I want to fight you, now. I want to kill you. *(His voice is still soft and terrible. The word "kill" is almost spit out.* FOOTS *does not move. He turns his head slightly to look* KAROLIS *in the eye, but he is motionless otherwise.)*

ORA: Goddamn it, fight!

He pushes KAROLIS *again. This time* KAROLIS *almost bumps* FOOTS *and* FOOTS *throws up his hands and pushes him away.*

FOOTS: Goddamn you! Goddamn you! *(His body moves from being completely immobile to an angry snarling figure.)* You bastard! *(The others become animated, clapping their hands, shouting, whistling, and moving around as if they were also fighting.)*

KAROLIS: No, Ray. I want to fight you. *(He is moving around now, but his hands are still held tightly and awkwardly at his sides.)* I want to fight you.

FOOTS *(moving around with his hands up to fight. They both move around each other and* FOOTS *seems to get momentarily, a change of heart)*: Look now, Karolis. . .you're just gonna get your head blocked.

KAROLIS *(as if he didn't hear)*: No. You have to fight me. I sent you a note, remember. That note saying I loved you. *(The others howl at this.)* The note saying you were beautiful. *(Tries to smile.)* You remember that note, Ray?

FOOTS: Goddamn it, if you're going to fight, fight you cocksucker!

KAROLIS: Yeh. That's what I'm going to do Ray. I'm going to fight you. We're here to fight. About that note, right? The one that said I wanted to take you into my mouth.

FOOTS *lunges at* KAROLIS *and misses.*

Did I call you Ray in that letter. . .or Foots? *(Trying to laugh.)* Foots! *(Shouts.)* I'm going to break your fucking neck. That's right. That's who I want to kill. Foots!

ORA *(pushing* KAROLIS *into* FOOTS*)*: Fight, you goddamn sissy-punk bastid!

FOOTS *(slaps* KAROLIS *with his open hand)*: You crazy bastard!

KAROLIS *(backing up. . .wanting to talk but still moving as if to fight)*: Are you Ray or Foots, huh?

The crowd begins to move forward to cut down the area of the match so that the two fighters will have to make contact.

HINES: Hit the sonofabitch, Foots!

FOOTS: Fight, you bastard!

KAROLIS: Yeh! That's why we're here, huh? I'll fight you, Foots! *(Spits the name.)* I'll fight you. Right here in this same place where you said your name was Ray. *(Screaming.*

He lunges at **FOOTS** *and manages to grab him in a choke hold.)* Ray, you said your name was. You said Ray. Right here in this filthy toilet. You said Ray. *(He is choking* **FOOTS** *and screaming.* **FOOTS** *struggles and is punching* **KAROLIS** *in the back and stomach, but he cannot get out of the hold.)* You put your hand on me and said Ray!

SKIPPY: Goddamn, that bastid is choking the shit out of Foots.

The two still struggle, with **KAROLIS** *continuing to have the advantage.*

HINES: That fuck is trying to kill Foots!

HOLMES: Goddamn it!

ORA *(suddenly leaping on Karolis' back, puts the same choke hold on him):* You cocksucka. . .how's that feel, huh? *(He pulls* **KAROLIS** *off of* **FOOTS** *who falls to his knees.)* Huh?

KNOWLES: Let's kick this cocksucka's ass real good.

He rushes up to help **ORA,** *and the whole of the crowd surges into the center punching the fallen* **KAROLIS** *in the face.* **KNOWLES** *is screaming with laughter.*

KAROLIS: No, no, his name is Ray, not Foots. You stupid bastards. I love somebody you don't even know.

He is dragged to the floor. The crowd is kicking and cursing him. **ORA** *in the center punching the fallen* **KAROLIS** *in the face.* **KNOWLES** *is screaming with laughter.*

FOOTS *is now on his hands and knees but his head hangs limply and he is unaware of what is happening. He slumps again.*

They have beaten **KAROLIS** *enough.* **KAROLIS** *is spread in the center of the floor and is unmoving.* **ORA** *drapes some of the wet toilet paper across his body and face.*

ORA: Let's stick the sonofabitch's head in the damn toilet.

PERRY: Oh, man, fuck you. The cat's completely out. What more can you do to him?

GEORGE: Yeh, let's get Foots, and get outta here before somebody comes in.

ORA: Yeh. Hee, hee. Look at ol' Foots. That fuckin' paddy boy almost kilt him.

LOVE: Yeh. *(Laughing.)* I told you Karolis was probably bad!

All laugh.

KNOWLES: Nutty sonofabitch.

LOVE *(picking up* **FOOTS,** *helped by* **HINES** *and* **HOLMES***)*: Hey, big eye! Get the hell up.

ORA *(takes a paper cup and dips it in the commode and throws it in Foots' face)*: Yeh, get up, bad ass. *(Laughs.)*

They all leave, as **FOOTS** *begins to come to. All making noise, laughing, cursing.* **KAROLIS** *lies as before in the center of the room, motionless.*

After a minute or so **KAROLIS** *moves his hand. Then his head moves and he tries to look up. He draws his legs up under him and pushes his head off the floor. Finally he manages to get to his hands and knees. He crawls over to* *one of the commodes, pulls himself up, then falls backward awkwardly and heavily. At this point, the door is pushed open slightly, then it opens completely and* **FOOTS** *comes in. He stares at Karolis' body for a second, looks quickly over his shoulder, then runs and kneels before the body, weeping and cradling the head in his arms.*

BLACK